Extraordinary Fish

Jb

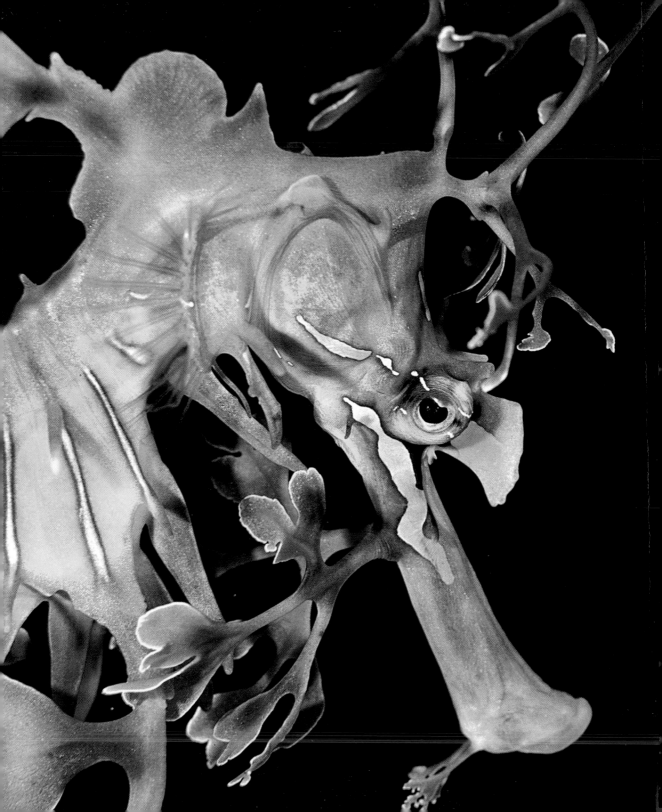

Extraordinary Fish

Frances Dipper

First published in 2001
BBC Worldwide Ltd,
Woodlands, 80 Wood Lane,
London W12 0TT

© BBC Worldwide Ltd 2001

ISBN 0 563 53409 5

Produced for BBC Worldwide by
Toucan Books Ltd, London

For BBC Worldwide
Commissioning editor:
Joanne Osborn
Editorial coordinator:
Patricia Burgess
Designer: Lisa Pettibone
Art director: Pene Parker

For Toucan Books
Commissioning editor:
Robert Sackville West
Editor: Molly Perham
Designer: Bob Burroughs
Picture researcher: Marian Pullen

Cover photograph: Mark
Garlick/Science Photo Library

Printed and bound in France by
Imprimerie Pollina s.a.
Colour separation by Kestrel
Digital Colour, Chelmsford

Contents

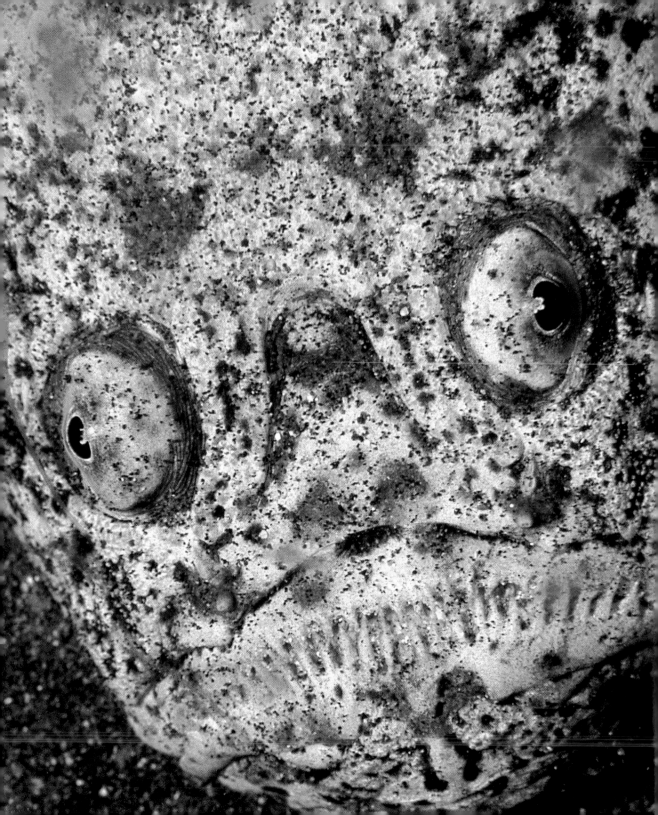

THE
WORLD OF
WEIRD FISH

THE WORLD OF WEIRD FISH

Among the 25,000 or so different species of fish, there are many that do not fit our idea of a typical fish. While it is easy to recognize familiar fish such as a cod or pike, some look so bizarre that it is difficult to think of them as fish at all. They have evolved weird shapes to suit their lifestyle and habitat, and to enable them to survive in a very competitive world. Some of the oddest-shaped fish live in difficult environments, such as the deep sea, where adaptations are necessary to cope with the extreme conditions. But weird shapes may also help in habitats such as coral reefs, where competition for resources is fierce and novel ways are needed to stay alive and make a living. Among the oddities are fish that breathe air using lungs, fish that are scaleless or armour-plated, fish that can live on land and even climb trees, and fish with fins that have become bizarre weapons, sensitive feelers or clinging suckers.

Previous page: The whitemargin stargazer has its bulbous eyes placed near the top of its head – one of the reasons behind its strange name.

BREAKING THE RULES

It was once thought that nothing could live in the inky black, ice-cold waters of the deep sea, where the pressure in the deepest parts can be 1000 times that at the surface. In fact, the deep sea is home to some of the most fascinating of all marine creatures – and to some particularly weirdly shaped fish.

Deep-sea gulper eels, distant relatives of river eels, are all mouth, with enormous jaws, thin slimy bodies and whip-like luminous tails. Food is hard to come by in these dark waters, so the huge mouth and a very elastic stomach allow these fish to eat whatever comes along, almost regardless of size. The majority of deep-sea fish that spend their lives wandering in mid-water are long and thin. Rat-tails or grenadiers are shaped rather like scaly tadpoles, and the largest species can reach 1.5 m (5 ft) long. These are the fish that have been filmed by ROVs (Remotely Operated Vehicles) swimming around the wreck of the *Titanic*.

Chimaeras, ancient relatives of the sharks that have been around for at least 400 million years, are found in most oceans down to around 2600 m

1. Most freshwater catfish are nocturnal, but the phantom glass catfish is active by day and makes a fascinating and easy-to-keep aquarium pet.

1. Despite its bizarre appearance, the elephant fish from Australia is good to eat and is caught by deep-sea trawlers.

2. Safe inside its box-like skeleton, this Hawaiian spotted trunkfish further deters predators by secreting a poison from its skin.

3. The long-horned cowfish searches for hidden invertebrates by blowing away the sand with a stream of water.

⭐ The greatest depth at which a fish has ever been caught is 8368 m (27,450 ft) in the Puerto Rico Trench. The 15-cm (6-in) long fish, called *Abyssobrotula galatheae*, was caught in 1970.

(8530 ft). They have such a bizarre appearance, they are often called ghost sharks or spook fish. Their thick heads are ridged by sensory canals that look like the sutures of a skull, and they have flabby, greyish bodies. The elephant fish is perhaps the weirdest of the species, with a long, trunk-like snout that it uses to plough through the bottom mud searching for food. But it is rivalled by the long-nosed chimaera, which carries the equivalent of a knight's jousting pole as a snout. In mythology, a chimaera was a monster with a lion's head, a serpent's tail and a goat's body. Fish chimaeras have some features from both bony fish and sharks, the two main groups of living fish, hence their name.

2

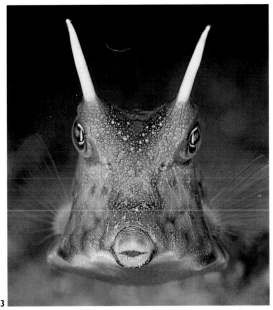

3

Boxed-in fish

Coral reef boxfish live within a suit of armour. They have no scales, but instead are encased in a rigid box of fused bony plates covered in brightly coloured skin so that they resemble animated Christmas presents. With such a stiff body, the only way they can swim is by beating their pectoral or side fins very rapidly, using their stubby tail like a rudder to help steer them. When seen head-on, the long-horned cowfish, a type of boxfish, looks like a bright yellow alien with two cow-like horns, bulbous green eyes and a small pouting mouth – no wonder most predators steer well clear! We know from the fossil record that some of the earliest fish were also heavily armoured with bony plates. Although this provided excellent protection, it also made them slow and clumsy.

BONELESS FISH

Eating a herring for supper can be a frustrating experience because it is full of small, sharp bones. But try eating a shark, such as dogfish (sold in the UK as 'huss' or 'rock salmon') and you won't find a single sharp bone. Sharks and their relatives, the rays and skates, belong to a class of fish called

Chondrichthyes or cartilaginous fish, whose skeleton is made almost entirely from lightweight, flexible cartilage. They are as different from the other main group of fish, the Osteichthyes or bony fish, as birds are from reptiles or mammals. Apart from the differences in their skeletons, their method of reproduction is also completely different and many bear live young (▷ p. 80). Shark have no

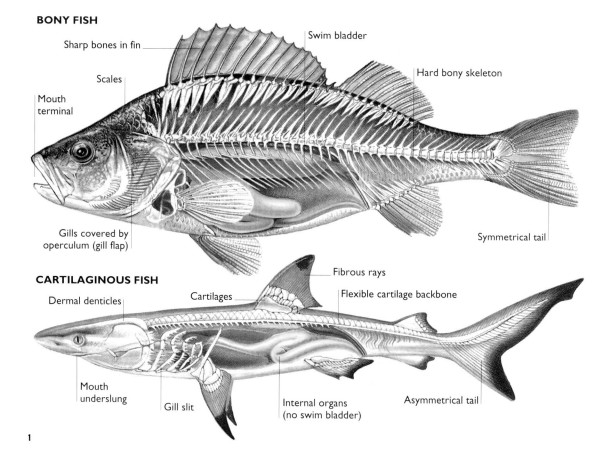

BONY FISH

- Sharp bones in fin
- Swim bladder
- Scales
- Hard bony skeleton
- Mouth terminal
- Gills covered by operculum (gill flap)
- Symmetrical tail

CARTILAGINOUS FISH

- Dermal denticles
- Cartilages
- Fibrous rays
- Flexible cartilage backbone
- Mouth underslung
- Gill slit
- Internal organs (no swim bladder)
- Asymmetrical tail

1

1. Some of the major differences in the skeleton and external features of bony and cartilaginous fish. Note also the lack of a swim bladder in the cartilaginous fish.

2. Shark skin is so tough and abrasive that in the past it was dried and tanned to form 'shagreen' and used to polish wooden objects.

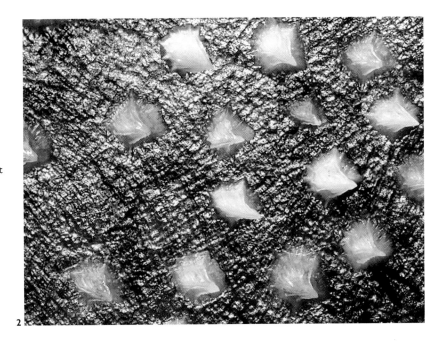

2

scales, but instead their skin is covered in tiny teeth called dermal denticles, giving it a sandpaper texture. There are only about 950 species of sharks and rays, but they are an incredibly successful group and have survived almost unchanged since they evolved from their bony fish ancestors around 450 million years ago.

Lords of the sea

Sharks are the top predators in the sea and, as such, have gained a largely undeserved reputation for ferocity. The great white shark is one of the largest, reaching at least 6 m (20 ft) and possibly 8 m (26 ft) long, and has been vilified as a man-eater. As is so

The fossil teeth from a prehistoric shark called *Megalodon* suggest that this giant was around 15 m (50 ft) long – at least twice the size of its close relative, the great white shark.

1

1. The great white shark is the world's largest living predatory fish.

2. The scalloped hammerhead shark is the commonest of the large hammerhead sharks. This one has parasites around its mouth.

often the case, the number of attacks is very small, and most are thought to be a case of mistaken identity – a human lying on a surfboard and paddling along looks like a turtle, and a diver in a black wetsuit resembles a seal – but the injuries inflicted can be horrific. The jaws are lined with rows of finely serrated, razor-sharp teeth. Those at the back gradually move forward and continuously replace worn and broken teeth: individual teeth may be replaced as often as every 8–15 days. When the shark attacks, it lifts its nose and the top jaw is pushed forward, exposing the teeth in a grisly smile before it clamps its jaws together.

Hammerhead sharks are easily the most extraordinarily shaped sharks, the head being flattened sideways into a wide, flat 'hammer' with an eye at each end. This gives the shark extremely

2

1. A manta ray swims gracefully through the clear waters around Hawaii. Like swifts in the air, mantas are almost continuously on the move, searching out the best feeding areas.

1

good, almost all-round, vision and provides more surface area on the head, increasing its sensory capacity, rather like the flattened base of a metal detector. These sharks have also been seen using the strangely shaped hammer head when attacking stingrays: they repeatedly batter their prey until it is sufficiently stunned for the shark to take a bite. Sometimes the stingrays lash out with their armoured tails – but the sharks do not seem to be affected by the poisonous stings that cause excruciating pain in humans.

Flattened sharks

Rays and skates are also cartilaginous fish: they are in effect flattened sharks adapted to a life on the seabed. Their pectoral or side fins have expanded to form wing-like structures with which they can swim gracefully through the water. The manta ray is the largest ray, with a wingspan of 5–7 m (16–23 ft). On either side of the mouth are two strange, pendulous flaps called cephalic lobes: it was these 'horns' and its whip-like tail that gave it the name of 'devilfish'.

Manta rays sometimes 'breach' like whales, throwing themselves up into the air, and this probably prompted their early reputation as attackers of boats and people. In reality, these gentle giants feed on plankton, and their ferocious 'horns' simply help to guide food into their huge mouths.

Giant rays also exist in fresh water. Recently the giant freshwater stingray has been discovered in a river in Sabah, northern Borneo. It also occurs in Thailand and Australia but is becoming extremely rare due to pollution and degradation of the rivers in which it lives. It looks like a huge living dinner plate up to 2 m (6 ft) across, with a small pointed nose and a long, whip-like tail with a ferociously long, stinging spine.

VITAL FINS

The one characteristic that almost all fish have in common is the possession of fins. Whatever their body shape and way of life, fish have to be able to swim, even if only for short distances. Most fish have a tail fin and other unpaired fins, plus paired pectoral (side) and pelvic (belly) fins. In predatory fish, such as the bluefin tuna, the fins are used to gain maximum speed and to give minimum drag, and this species can reach speeds of 70 km/h (45 mph). These sleek, fast fish have stiff, sickle-shaped tails, designed to give maximum thrust.

The speed record belongs to a relative of the tuna, the sailfish, which has been measured taking

 LIVING FOSSILS

In 1938, a few days before Christmas, the young curator of a small museum in South Africa was called down to the docks to collect some deep-sea fish from a trawler that had been fishing off the Comoros Islands. What she found eventually became one of the most celebrated of all fish. Nicknamed 'old four legs' because it had four limb-like fins, it was unlike any other fish known to science. Nearly 1.5 m (5 ft) long, it was covered in hard, plate-like scales and shone with iridescent colours. This was the coelacanth (right), a member of a group of fish previously thought to have been extinct for millions of years. In 1998 the fish again caused a sensation in zoological circles when another population was found, this time in deep water off Indonesia. A third population was found in 1999, at a depth of 107 m (350 ft), near Sodwana in South Africa. This time live video footage was obtained, but one diver died in the process of filming it. Scientists are still working on the question of whether these widely separated populations are the same species or not.

1

⭐ The young of the deep-sea black dragonfish has eyes on long stalks, which are up to half the length of its body. The stalks shorten as the fish grows, until the eyes end up in sockets.

out fishing line at a rate equivalent to around 110 km/h (70 mph). Sailfish are usually seen making spectacular leaps out of the water as they fight on the end of a fishing line. However, it is only under water that their extraordinary beauty is revealed. The dark, steel blue of their long, sleek body contrasts with the bright cobalt blue of the huge, sail-like dorsal fin after which they are named. This fin is used in courtship displays and is folded down into a groove when the fish is swimming fast.

The paired fins in bony fish are used mainly in manoeuvring and braking: they allow for great precision so that even in the crowded environs of a coral reef, collisions between fish are extremely rare. Sharks, on the other hand, cannot 'brake', so must swerve if a collision seems imminent. Sharks have relatively inflexible fins and cannot fold or bend them as bony fish can. Their large pectoral (side) fins are used to give lift and also act as hydroplanes to direct the shark up or down while it is swimming along.

Bony fish do not have to use their fins to give them lift because they evolved a special structure, the swim-bladder, a gas-filled balloon that provides buoyancy. It is this, plus the flexibility of the fins, that allows the infamous pike to hover almost motionless in mid-water as it stalks its prey. No shark can do this, and all sharks must swim to stay afloat, although some have enlarged, oily livers that help with their buoyancy.

Fanciful fins

The possession of a swim-bladder in bony fish means that not all the fins are needed for swimming and manoeuvring. Fins have developed into versatile and sometimes astonishing appendages used for defence, attack, feeding and courtship, as well as for novel ways of getting about. The prize for the most flamboyant fins must go to the Siamese fighting fish. The tail, dorsal and ventral fins of the males are larger than the fish itself and almost useless for swimming. The male displays his brightly coloured fins to the female in much the same way as a male peacock or a bird of paradise does to his potential mate. If the female shows no

1. Sailfish are difficult to observe under water as they live and hunt in the open ocean. This beautiful fish has been enticed into shot by using a bait ball.

2. A male Siamese fighting fish displays his flamboyant fins to a potential mate. The colours and size of fins in captive fish have been enhanced by selective breeding.

2

interest, the male often lives up to his name and she risks being attacked, as does any other male that tries to come near.

Fins can also be used to 'walk' or 'stand' on the seabed. The extraordinary tripod fish lives and hunts on the soft ooze of the deep-sea abyssal plains. To prevent itself sinking into the mud, it uses its elongated pelvic fins and tail as a tripod, and stands up on its fin tips. The curtain-like pectoral fins are then raised above its head like Dracula's cape as it waits patiently to ambush passing shrimps. In shallower water, gurnards and sea robins 'walk' across the seabed. The first three fin rays of their pectoral fins are modified as sensitive 'feet' with taste buds, and these are used to probe the sand for the small worms, crabs and sand eels on which they feed.

Coral reef frogfish also walk over the seabed: both sets of paired fins are modified to act as stout little 'legs', which they use either in alternate pairs like any other four-legged animal, or the pectoral fins are used in unison to haul the animal along. These ugly, warty, misshapen fish have no need to swim as they are well camouflaged: they simply crouch on the reef waiting to suck passing fish into their cavernous jaws. Many of these bottom-living fish have lost their swim-bladders, which are no longer of any use to them.

1. A red gurnard 'tiptoes' its way across the seabed in Brittany, France. If it detects an edible worm or crab with its sensitive 'feet', it will stop and dig it out with its armoured snout.

2. (opposite) These warty frogfish would be impossible to spot from any distance away. Matching their colour perfectly to the octocorals (coral-like animals) surrounding them, they remain motionless, hidden from predators and prey alike.

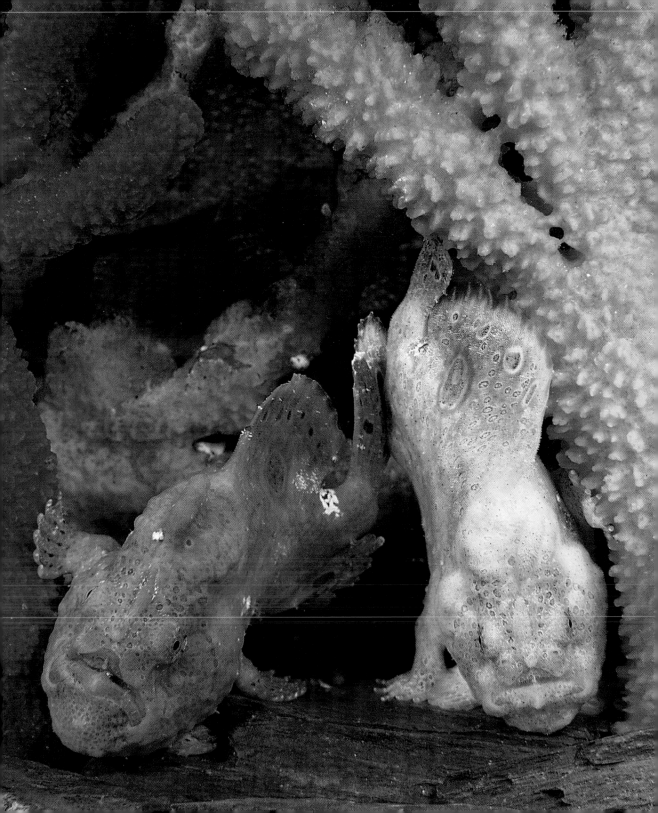

1

1. The Sargassum flying fish folds its large 'wings' away as it falls back into the water after escaping from a predator.

2. A male lumpsucker on guard duty at the nest site. The eggs would make tasty pickings for other fish and crabs if he neglected them. The eggs are also eaten by humans as lumpfish caviar.

Flying fish

While many fish, such as sailfish, manta rays and salmon, can leap out of the water, flying fish take things a step further. These small silvery fish live near the surface in tropical seas, and when chased by larger predatory fish, they will 'fly' to escape. The noise and vibrations from a speedboat will also make them take to the air. The pectoral fins are very large and wing-like and enable the fish to glide, but they cannot flap their 'wings'. Most species have only two wings but there are some four-winged species that use both pectoral and pelvic fins. As

they come out of the water, the best fliers keep the elongated lower half of their tail in the water and sweep it from side to side to continue building up speed. In this way they can sustain a glide of up to 200 m (650 ft), although most species achieve a distance of only 20–25 m (65–80 ft).

Hangers on

Fish that live in or near the seashore inhabit a turbulent world of crashing waves, where it is difficult to stay in one place. The strangely named lumpsucker has solved this problem by turning its pelvic fins into a powerful sucker. This is a temperate species found on cold and wild coasts around northern Europe. As its strange name suggests, this fish is covered in warty lumps and folds of skin, and even the dorsal fin becomes overgrown by skin as the fish matures. In late winter, the female attaches her cluster of eggs to rocks on or just below the seashore and then leaves the male to guard them. He will hang patiently on to the rocks with his strong sucker, even to the extent of being partly exposed as the tide recedes.

Sometimes, in a particularly bad storm, large numbers of these grotesque fish are washed off the rocks and cast ashore.

Pelvic fin suckers are also used by small fish that live in torrential streams and rivers, such as the hillstream loaches of Asia and the naked catfishes of the Andes. The latter also have a sucker-like mouth, so they can creep along against extremely strong currents and even climb waterfalls.

However, one group of fish, the remoras, has developed a sucker for quite another use. Remoras

2

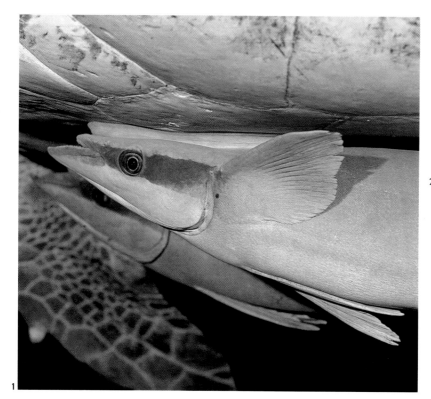

1. A turtle provides a ride for a remora. Remoras are also called shark suckers because they regularly attach themselves to sharks.

2. As a remora edges into place beneath its host, the ridges on its sucker are raised to displace water and create a strong suction.

A remora's sucker is so strong that the fish are sometimes tied on to lines by Asian fishermen and used to catch turtles and large fish.

are warm-water marine fish that appear to have strangely flattened and ridged heads reminiscent of the sole of a shoe. Their appearance results from the first dorsal fin, which is modified as an extremely efficient sucker. Remoras attach themselves to large animals, such as sharks, whales, dolphins and turtles, and literally hitch a ride. They can let go at any time to feed on scraps left by their hosts, and often change hosts, sometimes to the consternation of scuba divers, who become unwilling targets.

HOUSE HUNTING

The world of fish is truly vast: oceans, seas, lakes and rivers cover almost 80 per cent of the Earth and provide a huge variety of different watery habitats. Some fish have made themselves at home in extraordinary places, living and thriving in hot desert springs, ephemeral pools, underground rivers and lakes, and the icy depths of polar seas. Even the highest lake in the world, Lake Titicaca in the Andes, has its own populations of fish. Only one habitat has proved too difficult to conquer – the Dead Sea, which is just too salty.

Some fish, such as trout, which have been semi-domesticated by humans, are very widespread. Brown trout, which are native to Europe and western Asia, are now found on the other side of the world in New Zealand, the Falkland Islands and South America. By contrast, the devil's hole pupfish is found in only one small, hot pool in Death Valley, Nevada (USA), making it one of the rarest fish known. This is an example of an endemic species – that is, one found nowhere else. Lake Baikal is the oldest and deepest lake in the world and has more than 50 endemic fish species. The cichlid fishes of Africa's Rift Valley lakes have

3. A cichlid fish from Zambia prepares a shell as a nesting site. This is just one of very many African species.

3

diversified into hundreds of different species, each found only in one or several of the lakes. Like Darwin's famous Galapagos finches, these fish evolved apart, as lake levels changed, isolating each body of water. The brilliantly coloured orchid dottyback is an example of a marine endemic species from the Red Sea. Unlike the nearby Arabian Gulf, the Red Sea has a high number of endemic marine species because it was at one time isolated from the Indian Ocean for millions of years.

Volcanic fish

One of the most extreme environments on Earth is also home to several species of fish. Deep-sea vents are found 2000–3000 m (6500–10,000 ft) below the surface on parts of the mountainous mid-ocean ridges that run the length of all major oceans. These areas are volcanically active, and springs of hot water gush out of the vents at temperatures up to 400 °C. By contrast, the surrounding water is

1

1. The almost iridescent purple colour of the orchid dottyback make it a good photographic subject and a popular aquarium fish. It is endemic to the Red Sea.

2. Giant tube worms clustered round a volcanic vent at 2440 m (8000 ft) near the Galapagos Islands. Many strange deep-sea animals feed at these vents.

around 3–4 °C (37–39 °F). Since they were first filmed in 1977, these vents have proved to be a treasure-trove of bizarre animal life. Around the edges, in the cooler areas, giant tube worms, clams and shrimps abound, all ultimately dependent on special bacteria that manufacture food from the soup of chemicals dissolved in the vent water. Not surprisingly, several species of bizarre deep-sea fish, known as brotulids and eel-pouts, have been recorded around the vents, feeding on this animal bonanza. Very little is known about these fish, which have only recently been photographed from submersibles.

2

▷ SEA SERPENTS AND MONSTERS

There have always been tales of sea serpents and monsters, many undoubtedly the result of a trick of the light, combined with a fertile imagination. Early seafarers encountering the oarfish (juvenile, right) could be forgiven for dubbing it a sea serpent. This amazing fish – no photographs of living examples exist – has a flattened, snake-like body normally around 5–8 m (16–26 ft) long. It is the longest bony fish known. Its serpent-like appearance is accentuated by bright red fins, a flowing 'mane' of long fin filaments and a silvery, spotted body. Luckily, it is harmless and is thought to feed mainly on tiny planktonic animals.

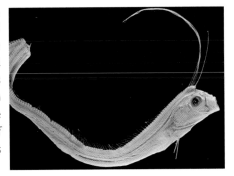

SURVIVAL

SURVIVAL

Survival in the cut and thrust of the fish world is a matter of skill and deception. The ultimate goal is to survive for long enough to reproduce successfully and so maintain population numbers. With the exception of a few top predators, such as the larger sharks, most fish face the everyday risk of becoming someone else's supper. All fish must eat, and to do so means coming out into the open to forage or hunt. Fish that inhabit the open sea face this exposure 24 hours a day. Such survival pressures have resulted in many ingenious methods for confusing predators and for enticing and catching prey. These methods include some truly bizarre adaptations in body form and colour, many aimed at camouflaging the fish to allow it to see while not being seen. The behaviour of camouflaged fish is also designed to lessen the likelihood of detection. Well-camouflaged fish tend to move very slowly and infrequently, but are capable of sudden bursts of great speed.

Previous page: The blotchy coloration and seaweed-like tassles on the head and body of the Sargassum fish provide it with excellent camouflage in its tangled seaweed home.

CAMOUFLAGE AND MIMICRY

Camouflage is widely used by fish, both to hide from predators and to confuse unsuspecting prey. The ultimate camouflaged predator is the Indo-Pacific coral reef stonefish: this is certainly among the ugliest of all fish, with its squashed head and craggy body covered in warts and tassels. As its name suggests, it is designed to look like a rock and can adapt its colour to suit the background. Divers have been known to stare these fish in the face and still not be able to see them. The fish keep still for such long periods of time that algae often grow on them, making them even more difficult to see.

Stonefish are expert ambush predators and can strike with incredible speed, sucking unsuspecting small fish into their cavernous mouths. The fish itself is protected from attack by larger predators, not only by its camouflage, but also because it has extremely poisonous fin spines. Humans are stung when they tread on the fish in shallow water and the sting is incredibly painful and can be fatal.

As camouflage experts go, the leafy sea dragon, found off the coasts of south Australia, should also win a prize. This time the aim is concealment from predators, and the chosen template is seaweed. Sea dragons are closely related to seahorses and pipefish. All these fish have very long snouts, and

1. A reef stonefish squats like an ugly toad on the seabed, waiting for its next victim to swim past.

stiff bodies encased in protective bony plates: their shape and body armour mean that they cannot move fast, so camouflage is essential. The head and the whole body are decorated with long, seaweed-like skin tassels, which effectively break up their outline: even out in the open, their leisurely movements give them the appearance of a piece of drifting seaweed.

Over on the other side of the world in the North Atlantic, the Sargasso-fish, a type of frogfish, spends its entire life crawling through the huge rafts of floating *Sargassum* seaweed that drift across the ocean. It, too, has tassels of loose skin, and ragged fins that help conceal it in its seaweed home as it hunts for small shrimps.

Fish chameleons

Most fish that rely heavily on camouflage, as the stonefish does, have at least some ability to change colour to suit their background. This ability is developed to an extraordinary degree in some flatfish, such as the Mediterranean flounder. These fish normally live on sand, gravel or shingle on the sea floor, and they can alter the spottiness and colour of their skin to suit their current back-ground within just a few seconds. When placed on a chessboard background in an experimental tank, they are able to make a very good attempt at matching the black and white squares, but as it is an unfamiliar background, it takes them longer.

1. This long-spined sea scorpion has taken on a predominantly red coloration to match its backdrop of red sponges and seaweeds.

2. Shrimpfish swim in small shoals, and if disturbed will glide away as a group, still in their head-down posture.

1

The little, long-spined sea scorpion, found in rock-pools around Britain, is red and pink in pools with red seaweed and a dull brown and grey when hiding under brown kelp or bladder wrack seaweed. On the East Anglian coast, where the rock-pools are lined with chalk, these little fish are almost white in colour.

False pretences

Extra protection is gained by some fish that not only camouflage themselves, but also adjust their behaviour to make their disguise more authentic. The seagrass filefish lives in seagrass beds and among mangrove roots. In colour and shape it already resembles a large leaf, and, if frightened, allows itself to drift around like a dead leaf.

Shrimpfish have long, pointed snouts and flattened, razor-like bodies. Although they can swim horizontally, they prefer to swim in a head-down posture in small groups so that they resemble waving seagrass or soft corals. This posture also helps them to hide among the spines of black sea urchins, where their dark, horizontal stripes are held vertical and so appear like urchin spines.

Protection by deception

Pretending to be something you are not is a useful way to gain protection or to deceive prospective prey. This strategy is taken to extremes by the sabre-toothed mimic blenny. In colour, shape and size it closely resembles the blue streak cleaner wrasse, a common resident of tropical reefs.

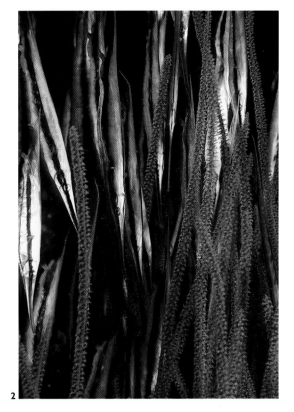

2

At night parrotfish wrap themselves in a mucus cocoon and go to sleep in a rock crevice. The mucus prevents predators from smelling them.

The little striped wrasse is almost never attacked by other large fish because it performs the very useful function of picking parasites off the skin and gills of its hosts. The blenny uses its disguise to approach larger fish and then, instead of cleaning them, it takes a bite out of their fins, skin or scales – a very unwelcome surprise. The mimic filefish, on the other hand, pretends to be dangerous when it is not.

It closely resembles the black-saddled pufferfish, which, like most puffers, has poisonous flesh and is avoided by predators. Some tropical snake eels are spotted or striped and look like venomous sea snakes. Divers on holiday in the Red Sea sometimes report having seen sea snakes: in most cases they have been deceived by a sneaky snake eel, as true sea snakes are absent from the Red Sea.

2

1. and 2. The resemblance between the cleaner wrasse, seen here cleaning an oriental sweetlips (left), and the mimic blenny (above) is striking.

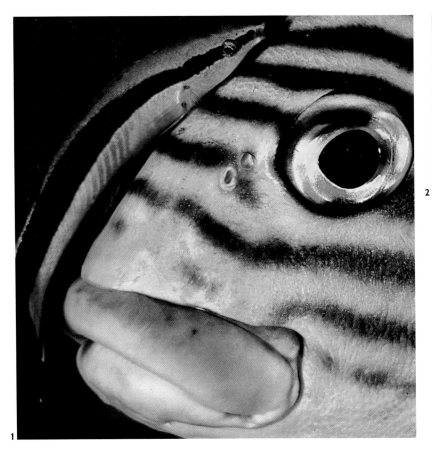

1

SPINES, KNIVES AND POISONS

While many fish rely on camouflage for protection, or physically hide away from predators, others arm themselves with a battery of different weapons. At least 40 different species of fish are known that have venomous spines of one sort or another.

Surgeonfish are peaceful grazers on coral reefs and appear as the most unlikely assassins. Active mainly at dusk, these colourful fish can be seen busily picking at rocks and corals, their chisel-like teeth scraping off the algae on which they feed. However, if a predator approaches, the fish quickly arm themselves by snapping out a moveable spine on each side of the tail stalk. Lashing the tail from side to side, they can inflict a nasty wound with these scalpel-like blades. Inquisitive divers beware!

In the unicornfish there are two or three non-retractable blades, and the fish looks intimidating

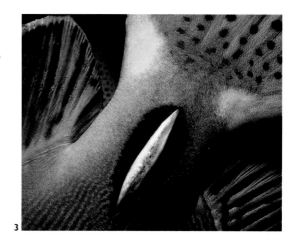

3

3. The sheathed 'knife' of an eyestripe surgeonfish, shows up clearly against the yellow tailbase of the fish.

 SHOCK TACTICS

Fish are the only vertebrates that can produce electricity and use it, both as a weapon and for catching prey. Of the 250 or so species with this ability, only a few can produce a really powerful discharge. The electric eel (right) is one of these. It lives in murky rivers in South America and can grow to at least 2 m (6 ft) long. A fish this size can produce a discharge of up to 550 volts, sufficient to stun quite large prey fish and kill smaller ones. The eel has large electrical organs, which can make up half its bulk, and which contain banks of special disc-like cells arranged in tubes. Potential predators, or animals or humans wading in the river and coming into contact with an electric eel, can be severely shocked.

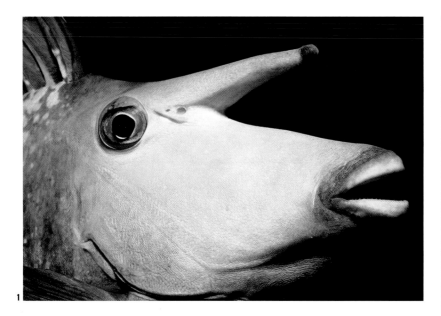

because it has its nose drawn out into a long 'unicorn' horn. The 'scalpels' are highly modified body scales.

When porcupinefish are out hunting the small sea urchins, snails and crabs that they relish, they carry their body cover of spines flat, just as their namesake does. However, if attacked by a predator, they can suck in large amounts of water and so inflate themselves into an extraordinarily prickly ball. As if that weren't enough, some species have body markings that swell into glaring 'eyes' when they inflate themselves. Unfortunately, this show of strength does not put off human predators, and the inflated fish are often sold as souvenirs.

Surgeonfish and porcupinefish rarely come into contact with humans, but there are other armed

1. The function of the long 'horn' in unicornfish is probably to intimidate predators. In this bluespine unicornfish the horn is only moderately long. In other species it can be longer than the snout, making feeding difficult.

2. Another name for the porcupinefish is the balloonfish. Once inflated, it can swim only slowly and must rely on its spines to deter predators.

1. A blue-spotted stingray, disturbed from its resting place on a Red Sea coral reef, skims away over the sand.

2. (opposite) The spotfin lionfish hunts by night, usually spending the day under ledges and in holes in the coral.

species that do. Stingrays are perhaps the most notorious. Each ray is armed with one or more serrated spines on its long, flexible tail. If trodden on by a human, or attacked by a predator, the ray will lash out with its tail. Divers on coral reefs may come into contact with the blue-spotted stingray, which hides under coral heads and in sandy patches.

In Great Britain and Europe, bathers are sometimes stung by weeverfish, one of a large number of fish that use their spiny fins as protective weapons. Like stingrays, weevers lie partly buried in the sand, but in this case it is the first dorsal fin that carries the poisonous spines. With the exception of the stonefish, fish stings are rarely fatal, but most are excruciatingly painful and medical treatment should always be sought. The toxins affect the nervous system and can cause fainting, palpitations, vomiting and respiratory distress. If the wound is treated quickly with very

hot water, the pain subsides because heat inactivates the venom. Secondary infection of the wound can still be a problem, however.

Self-defence

The majority of armed fish carry their weapons purely for self-defence. Unlike snakes, which use their venomous bite to capture prey, poisonous fish react only if provoked. Most are also camouflaged, which makes them more dangerous to humans. The flamboyant lionfish, however, uses a different strategy and advertises the fact that predators would be well advised to leave it in peace. Like its relatives the stonefish and scorpionfish, the lionfish carries a deadly arsenal of poisonous fin spines. Unlike them, it is brightly coloured and its long fin spines are decked out in red, white and black, like bunting on a carnival float.

THE ART OF FEEDING

Getting enough to eat, without being eaten yourself, is a basic skill necessary for survival. Fish exhibit a great variety of feeding strategies. Predators such as the great white shark are well known and feared for their hunting skills. Others, such as surgeonfish on coral reefs and carp in ponds, are herbivores that graze on algae, seaweed or aquatic plants. Deep-sea grenadier fish scavenge off dead carcasses that have drifted down into the depths. However, some fish have developed their feeding skills to an extraordinary degree.

In the slow backwaters of a tropical river, a cricket sits quietly on a branch overhanging the river. Suddenly, a high-speed jet of water knocks it off its perch and into the water. It hardly has time to struggle before it disappears beneath the surface. The cricket has become dinner for an archerfish.

1

 PLANKTON EATERS

Floating in the sunlit surface waters of the oceans are microscopic plants and animals, the plankton. Tiny plants generate food for tiny animals, which in turn are eaten by small fish, shrimps and others. Plankton thus forms the basis for most aquatic life. However, it is a strange paradox that the largest fish in the sea, the whale shark, feeds directly on the tiniest plants and animals, the plankton. Whale sharks can reach 14 m (46 ft) in length, and their massive bulk is sustained entirely by sieving plankton out of sea water using modified gills. At the other end of the scale, on coral reefs, clouds of small orange 'goldfish', or *Anthias*, pick invisible plankton from the water, like swallows swooping after tiny insects. This 'wall of mouths' is extremely efficient, scooping up much of the available plankton.

1. With incredible accuracy, an archerfish squirts a mouthful of water and brings down an insect off a branch in an Indonesian jungle.

2. A common saw shark resting on the seabed. These fish live sluggish lives, rooting in the mud for invertebrates.

Pages 42–3: *Anthias* feed on plankton on a coral reef.

These small fish can squirt a stream of water out of their mouths that is strong enough to sting a person's face. They are extremely accurate within a range of about 1 m (3 ft), but can hit targets up to 3 m (10 ft) away. This is a remarkable achievement, as the fish have to take into account the distortion caused by looking up out of one medium, water, into another, air. Light waves are bent when they enter water, so an accurate aim is no easy task.

The 'four-eyed' fish of Central and South America can focus simultaneously both above and below water. In reality they have only two eyes, but each is divided horizontally into an upper and lower section. By swimming along at the water's surface with the lower half of each eye submerged and the upper half in the air, they can look out for predators and prey both above and below the water.

Heads or tails

Unlike archerfish, which stay mostly at the surface, sawfishes and saw sharks live on the bottoms of estuaries, rivers and coastal flats. Their problem is finding prey that is well hidden in sand and mud. Sawfishes, which are specialized rays, are famous for their incredibly long, flat, bony snouts edged with teeth, resembling a two-edged saw. This fearsome-looking weapon is used to search out and stun or kill their hidden prey, mostly invertebrates and bottom-living fish. The greater sawfish can grow to nearly 8 m (26 ft) long, but such large fish are almost never seen nowadays. This species has been heavily over-exploited both for food and because the saws fetch high prices as souvenirs. Saw sharks are even better than sawfishes at ▷▷

2

⭐ Megamouth, a 5-m (16-ft) long giant shark, first discovered in 1976, has luminous jaws. These may help attract the tiny plankton shrimps on which it feeds in the depths.

their body, measuring up to 1.5 m (5 ft). These fish often hunt in groups or pairs. The sharks locate a shoal of fish and then swim round and round, 'herding' them with their tails. Their tails are then used as a weapon and whipped from side to side to stun and kill their prey.

Meat-eaters and vampires

While sharks have a reputation as fearsome predators in the oceans, piranhas have an equally bad reputation in rivers, enhanced by their regular appearances in James Bond films. The common red-bellied piranha has the worst reputation, resulting from its ability to strip a large animal, such as a deer (or a human), down to a skeleton in just a few minutes. However, such feeding frenzies are rare and are usually sparked by blood in the

finding buried crabs, worms and fish: their 'saw' is adorned with extremely sensitive barbels, like multiple moustaches, which feel and taste their prey.

Thresher sharks use their tails, rather than their snouts, to stun their prey. These sleek sharks live out in the open oceans, where they hunt for shoals of fish. Their extraordinary tail is nearly as long as

1. The hagfish or sea lamprey is parasitic and uses its disc-like sucker mouth to hang firmly on to its prey and to rasp a hole in its side.

2. The fearsome teeth of a meat-eating piranha. These fish sometimes meet an ignominious end, being dried and encased in Perspex as souvenirs for tourists.

2

water, as is the case with sharks. The large Amazonian piranha grows up to 60 cm (2 ft) long and has strong, razor-sharp teeth that meet and interlock exactly. People have safely swum with these animals, but, as with large sharks, they should always be treated with the utmost respect. Many other species of piranhas are vegetarian or eat other fish.

A more circumspect approach is taken by the strangely named cookie-cutter shark. This small, cigar-shaped shark sucks on to tuna and other large fish, dolphins or whales. It then sticks its large, razor-sharp lower teeth into its victim and twists around until it has cut out a plug of flesh. The shark seems even more vampire-like because it glows an eerie luminescent green in the dark, possibly to attract predators that it then attacks itself.

Eel-like lampreys and hagfish attach themselves to larger animals by their sucker-like mouth, and then rasp away the flesh of their victim with circular rows of horny teeth. These fish have no proper jaws and in this respect are similar to the oldest-known fossil fish, which date back about 530 million years and were recently found by scientists working in China.

SURVIVING HOSTILE ENVIRONMENTS

Fish that live in extreme environments have to take extreme measures to survive. This has resulted in the evolution of some very strange fish with adaptations that enable them to live in either the hottest or coldest places on Earth.

In Africa, South America and Australia, many flood-plain lakes, pools, swamps and even rivers evaporate in the dry season. The water becomes increasingly warm, muddy and devoid of oxygen, conditions under which most fish would die rather quickly. Lungfish overcome this by breathing air: coming to the surface at regular intervals, they take a gulp of air before disappearing again with a twist of their eel-like bodies. Some species also have rudimentary gills, but only the Australian lungfish can use these to breathe: the others have to breathe air, even when they are living in well-oxygenated water. Lungfish were common around 380 million years ago and may have been among the ancestral stock from which land-living animals evolved. The young larval stages of the Australian lungfish look very like amphibian tadpoles.

Hibernating fish

On land, animals as diverse as polar bears and tortoises can go into a state of torpor and hibernate through the cold of winter. Some species of African lungfish can also become torpid, but they do so to

1

1. The Australian lungfish has gills as well as lungs. Unlike other lungfish, it cannot survive in dried-out pools.

2. The mucus cocoon of an African lungfish, in which it can remain dormant for months or even years, until the rains return to fill the pool.

3. In the freezing waters of the Antarctic, an icefish cruises slowly along.

2

survive the heat, not the cold. Before the fierce African sun bakes their pools completely dry and the mud at the bottom hardens, the fish dig bulb-shaped burrows in the mud and coil up in the bottom. When there is hardly any water left, they secrete large amounts of sticky mucus. With the water finally gone, the cocoons dry out to form the equivalent of a plastic bag, in which the fish stays moist and comfortable. As they have lungs, they can breathe through a small tube to the outside. The body metabolism of the lungfish slows right down and it can survive on its fat reserves for several months, or even years, until the rains return.

Refrigerated fish

Fish living in the icy cold waters of the Southern Ocean surrounding Antarctica face a very different problem, that of freezing to death. The cold itself is not the problem, but the fish must prevent themselves being frozen because ice crystals disrupt living cells. In the coldest areas, the temperature of Antarctic sea water can fall to -1.9 °C (30 °F) before it freezes. This is below the temperature at which the blood of most fishes would freeze. In the early days of whaling, fishermen told tales of a ghostly white fish with a head like a crocodile, which could survive being frozen into the ice. This particular fisherman's tale turned out to be true. Crocodile icefish are very pale because their blood has no red blood cells and is therefore almost colourless. This lack of haemoglobin, which is a rather viscous substance, helps the blood to flow freely in cold conditions. The fish manages perfectly well without haemoglobin because cold water carries a large amount of oxygen. It is also rather sluggish by nature, and does not need much oxygen to survive. In addition, scientists have discovered that icefish blood contains a natural glycoprotein 'antifreeze'. This acts in just the same way as the antifreeze in a car radiator, by lowering the freezing point of the blood.

3

PERSECUTION

For millions of years, fish have been evolving in body form, behaviour and reproductive strategies to help them survive and to maintain a balance between predators and prey. For most of human history, humans were part of this balance and had little impact on fish populations. Today all that has changed, and humans now pose by far the greatest threat to the survival of many species. Efficient, modern fishing methods have caused fish stocks all over the world to collapse. Cod in Newfoundland, herring in the North Sea, sardines in California – stocks of all these fish collapsed due to over-fishing, and none have recovered their original state.

1

TOTAL WORLD CATCH

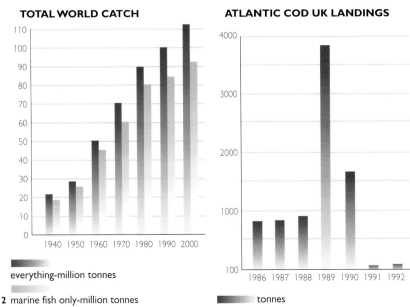

everything-million tonnes

2 marine fish only-million tonnes

ATLANTIC COD UK LANDINGS

tonnes

1. This school of Atlantic cod are being held in a fish pen in Norway. With the decline in wild stocks, attempts are being made to farm cod and other popular edible fish.

2. More and more fish have been caught worldwide every year, but many stocks, such as Atlantic cod, have been overfished and landings have declined sharply.

3. Cyanide fishermen wear hoods as protection against the poison they are unleashing to stun reef fish.

The Atlantic cod will eat almost anything, from bottom-living fish to shellfish, crabs, worms and sea urchins. This means that it can live over a wide variety of seabed habitats. It produces huge numbers of eggs: a really large adult can lay 9 million eggs a year. Cod can live for at least 20 and possibly 30 years. It can survive very low water temperatures and is resistant to disease and parasites. Cod was once one of the most abundant fish in any ocean. It was especially common off the coast of North America, and salt cod, along with molasses and slaves, were all linked in trade in the mid-1600s. Today the unthinkable has happened, and cod is becoming an expensive luxury, the victim of our too successful fishing methods.

New species

New species of fish are still being discovered. A rare river shark called *Glyphis* was discovered in Sabah, Borneo, in 1996, and at least one other new shark was found by the same team. However, this and many other species are threatened by habitat destruction, and new species may well become extinct before they have even been documented. Coral reef fish populations in Malaysia, Indonesia and the Philippines are suffering badly from dynamite fishing, which destroys the reefs on which they depend. Cyanide is also used to catch live fish for the aquarium trade, but corals are often damaged or killed in the process.

3

SENSES AND SIGNALLING

SENSES AND SIGNALLING

Fish communicate with each other in many different ways and for a variety of reasons: finding and attracting a mate, warning off rivals, and staking out a territory are prime examples. Others include scaring off predators and keeping together in groups or shoals. Water is a very different medium from air, and its properties affect how fish communicate. Underwater visibility, even in the clearest tropical seas, can never be as good as it is on land. While an eagle can rely on its eyesight alone to spot potential prey, sharks and other predatory fish supplement eyesight with their acute senses of smell and hearing, and ability to detect vibrations. Sound carries extremely well in water, travelling nearly five times as fast as it does in air. Human ears are not designed to cope with this, and scuba divers find it very hard to locate the source of an underwater noise. Some fish, however, have acute directional hearing.

Previous page: The milletseed or lemon butterflyfish is one of many similar species found around Hawaii. The fish recognize each other by subtle differences in their patterns.

NOT SO SILENT WORLD

In 1953 Captain Jacques Cousteau wrote *The Silent World*, his famous book about his underwater experiences as an early scuba diver. It is now clear that the sea is anything but a silent place. Scientists with hydrophones have recorded the equivalent of the 'dawn chorus' on coral reefs, as night gives way to day and the fish change shifts. Most of these rather inarticulate noises are produced by using a gas-filled swim-bladder as an amplifier. The swim-bladder is normally used to provide the fish with buoyancy. Gurnards, toadfishes and croakers, for example, have special muscles that they use to resonate their modified swim-bladders. Fish that make such noises also tend to have better hearing than those that do not, and have a connection between the ear and the swim-bladder that amplifies the sound.

Top of the pops

Toadfish, or midshipmen, are some of the noisiest fish in the sea. They are rather ugly, slimy fish with a flattened head, wide mouth and large, bulbous eyes. Their unappealing shape is, however, ideally suited to a passive life spent hiding under rocks. When it comes to courtship, these sluggish animals sing a nocturnal serenade that is quite unsurpassed. Males excavate a nest, usually underneath a rock, and entice females in with a series of growls, grunts and even whistles. People who live on boats in

1. Unsupecting fishermen have been known to drop their catch when they come across the oyster toadfish, which grunts loudly when handled.

California sometimes complain that the noise is so loud it keeps them awake. A toadfish called the Atlantic midshipman sings particularly well, but also impresses potential partners by lighting up a series of bioluminescent spots along both sides. These look rather like shiny buttons on a naval uniform, which is why they are called 'midshipmen'. Toadfish will also grunt loudly at other times, including when they are handled by fishermen.

Male thornback cowfish also serenade their chosen mates. On calm evenings in spring, the small males swim rapidly around the females, showing off their bright colours. Each couple then swims up near to the surface and the male hums loudly to the female before they spawn.

1

Croakers, or drums, are unremarkable-looking fish with remarkable vocal talents. They can creak, drum, purr, hum and whistle, rapidly repeating the sounds. It is even thought that the song of the Sirens in Greek mythology might have been based on the cacophony of noise produced by shoals of these fish. Similarly, the North American freshwater drum makes noises loud enough to be heard from a canoe, and features in local legends. Many live in murky coastal waters and estuaries where visibility is low, so sound communication becomes more important.

Sound is also important at night, when vision is of limited use. Nocturnal fish, such as the west Atlantic jackknife fish, another member of the drum family, use sound. This black and white species has an extremely long dorsal fin that it carries around like a banner, which may serve to make predators think it is bigger than it really is. Gurnards are nocturnal fish found in European coastal waters that communicate with short, sharp grunts interspersed by lengthy silences.

Basic sounds can also be made by fish without using the swim-bladder. The giant ocean sunfish makes a grating noise by grinding together a set of teeth in its throat (called the pharangeal teeth). These huge, almost circular fish spend their solitary lives out in the open ocean, feeding largely on jellyfish, and may use sound to make contact with potential mates.

Fish, such as the bullhead, which has spiny gill covers and fins, can make noises by rubbing these against other parts of the body, rather like a cricket does with its legs and wing covers.

1. The jackknife fish lives in the Caribbean, hiding in coral crevices. It emerges at night, when its dramatic stripes provide camouflage.

2. The sunfish can grow to 3 m (10 ft) and may weigh up to 1500 kg (3300 lb). Maximum size is difficult to substantiate as they are rarely caught.

CITY LIGHTS

On land, colour is widely used in the animal and plant kingdoms as an avenue of communication: flowers have bright colours to attract pollinating insects, while the vivid patterns of, for example, poison arrow frogs warn off potential predators. In the underwater world, light is quickly absorbed by water, especially in coastal waters thick with suspended silt particles or dense plankton blooms, so bright colours are only of use in shallow, well-lit habitats, such as coral reefs. Healthy coral reefs are crowded places, and here colour communication is taken to extremes. The Picasso triggerfish is a good example and looks, as its name suggests, like the efforts of an imaginative abstract painter. The magnificent emperor angelfish is one of the larger coral reef fish and is patterned with bright blue and yellow stripes with a black, white and blue face mask. These colours ensure each species can recognize its own kind in the crowd. This is particularly important in a group such as the butterflyfish where, on a healthy reef, there may be as many as a dozen different species all with much the same

1. The dark stripe across the eye of this Picasso triggerfish in the Red Sea may confuse predators as to which way it is swimming.

2. The juvenile of the emperor angelfish has a completely different colour pattern from the adult (seen here) – a dark blue body with white, circular stripes.

body shape. Distinctive colour patterns within a species also help fish tell the sex of other individuals. This helps prevent confusion among themselves, but certainly causes problems for biologists.

Deceptive colours

One of the problems encountered by reef fish is that their bright patterns may be seen not only by potential mates, but also by potential predators. It is difficult for humans to imagine how such colourful fish could ever blend into the background. However, the contrasting stripes displayed by many reef fish, such as the emperor angelfish, merge together when seen at a distance, so the fish can use their bright colours to signal potential mates at close quarters while remaining invisible to predators further away.

2

 COLOUR CONFUSION

Water quickly absorbs light so that deeper areas are much darker than the shallows, but it also changes the balance of colour in the light. Underwater photographers know that if they take photographs of lionfish using natural light, the fish will appear blue or grey: the beautiful red coloration will be restored only if a flash is used with the camera. Similarly, a diver who cuts himself under water will bleed 'blue' blood. Sunlight is made up of all the colours of the rainbow, and as the light penetrates the water, the red end of the spectrum is absorbed first, so bright red colours appear some shade of blue through to black. Nocturnal fish such as squirrelfish and soldierfish (right) can take advantage of this. During the day they hide in dark crevices and caves, and in the poor light their red coloration provides them with good camouflage, especially as most fish cannot see red colours at all well. Some deep-water fish are red for the same reason.

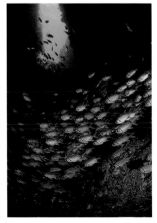

Fish can also see in the ultraviolet range, which is visible only at very close quarters and so makes a very good private signal. In the past, the intricate, striped patterns of some fish have been interpreted by local fishermen as signs from a higher being. The tail pattern of one semicircle angelfish in a Zanzibar market resembled Arabic letters that were interpreted as reading 'there is no god but Allah'.

Bioluminescence

At night ships display particular patterns of lights to indicate their size and which direction they are sailing in. Correct interpretation of these signals is vital to avoid collisions. In the perpetual darkness of deep ocean waters, fish use bioluminescence to communicate with each other in a similar way. Patterns of light help fish to recognize potential mates, avoid predators and even lure prey within their reach. Males and females of the same species often have slightly different patterns of lights, in the same way that shallow-water fish show a sexual dimorphism of colours. The eerie greenish bioluminescent light is produced from a chemical called luciferin, manufactured in special light organs. This is oxidized or 'burnt' with the help of another chemical, a catalyst called luciferase, to release energy in the form of cold light.

The deep-water anglerfish *Gigantactis* uses its bioluminescent powers to mislead smaller fish and entice them close enough to be grabbed by its fang-like teeth and eaten. This fish has its snout drawn out into an enormously long, thin 'fishing rod' with a bioluminescent lure at the end. This is waggled

enticingly to look like a luminescent shrimp or other small prey. Eel-like dragonfish have a luminescent barbel on the lower jaw that serves a similar purpose. Many of these fearsome predators are quite small, mostly under 30 cm (12 in) or so long. Larger predators would find it hard to catch sufficient food in these inky black waters.

Loose-jaws, or wide-mouths, have two light organs under their eyes, the smaller of which emits a normal bluish bioluminescence and is used for recognition purposes. The larger organ produces an unusual, deep red bioluminescent light. Just as humans cannot see a beam of light in the infrared range, this red light is invisible to the shrimps on which the loose-jaws feed. The unsuspecting shrimps are spotlighted and quickly eaten.

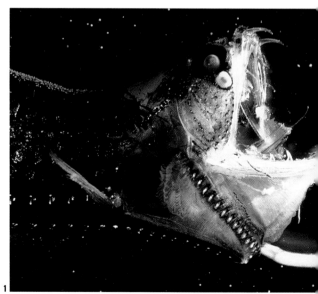

1

1. Dragonfish have lines of photophores, miniature light-producing organs, along the belly and head, and a bioluminescent chin barbel. They can be found as deep as 2000 m (6500 ft).

2. The luminous fishing rod on the head of this female deep-water anglerfish lures other fish within reach of its cavernous mouth and fang-like teeth.

2

▷ BACTERIAL SLAVES

Flashlight fish (right) live in deep water but swim up on to shallow coral reefs at night to feed. Beneath each eye they have a large, bioluminescent light organ, which can be turned off by pushing it down under a flap of skin. The fish turn the lights on and off every 5–10 seconds, and as they move slowly around, the shoals of fish look like underwater fireflies. The light is not made by the fish themselves, but by captive bacteria cultured in special sacs. The bacteria are present in huge numbers – up to 10 billion per cubic cm – and get all their food from the fish. The bizarre Australian pineapplefish (below) has similar light organs on its lower jaw, which it uses to help it feed. Its rounded body is completely encased in large, thick, protective scales, which are yellow outlined in black and armed with spines.

1. A school of flashlight fish in an Indonesian shipwreck. **1**

BODY LANGUAGE

Using special breathing equipment, humans are able to visit the underwater world and observe its inhabitants. However, with a face mask covering their eyes and nose, and breathing through a demand valve in their mouths, divers are effectively gagged. Communication must be by way of hand signals and body language. Fish, too, use body language to communicate under water, to each other, and occasionally to visiting humans as well. A small anemonefish swimming up to a diver's mask and waggling its fins in annoyance at an intrusion into its territory is amusing, but ignoring a grey reef shark lifting its snout, arching its back and lowering its pectoral (side) fins would be extremely foolhardy. The shark is telling the diver, or other shark, that it feels threatened or annoyed and may attack.

Home defences

Such stereotyped behavioural signals are relatively common among fish, especially in territorial disputes. Fish generally hold territories in order to provide a safe area in which eggs can be laid and guarded. Clear signals are needed, both to attract mates into the territory and to keep rivals out.

1

1. Two male mudskippers duel with each other. The one on the left is backing down and will wriggle away.

2. A mudskipper keeps a lookout from its perch on a branch of a mangrove tree, safe from water-bound predators. It will drop quickly back into the water if threatened by a bird or reptile.

2

Mudskippers are expert at such semaphore signals, but these strange fish do all their communicating out of the water. With goggle-eyes set high on the top of their heads, these little fish can keep a good lookout over the waterlogged mud-flats on which they live. Several species of mudskipper are common among the mangrove trees found along many tropical shorelines. When the tide goes out, they wriggle across the wet mud searching for tiny animals and plant material to eat. If danger threatens, they can also 'skip' rapidly across the mud by curving their bodies and pushing down with their tail, which acts as a spring. Breathing is not a problem because they frequently dip into pools and fill their gill chambers with water. They also take in some air, which oxygenates the water sloshing around over their gills.

If a rival male comes into another's territory, the two opponents engage in a silent, face-to-face match. Each lifts up its head and opens its mouth wide to try to intimidate the other. Usually this is sufficient for the smallest or weakest to back down. The winner then flags his victory by raising his dorsal fins. When it comes to enticing a female to spawn in his nesting burrow, the male uses his whole body to signal his intent. As well as raising his brightly coloured dorsal fins, he shows off his athletic prowess by leaping a short distance into the air, using his powerful tail. If the female is suitably impressed, she enters the nest burrow and spawns, closely followed by the male, who fertilizes the egg mass. Some species of these extraordinary fish can even climb the trees in their mangrove home by using a sucker derived from their pelvic (belly) fins.

LIVING TOGETHER

Safe living space is at a premium in the sea, where predators abound. Living with a partner can overcome some of these problems, but good communication between the partners is essential for success. On coral reefs an extraordinary relationship has evolved between small bottom-living fish called gobies and a type of shrimp known as alpheids. These strange partners are found living together in burrows in sandy areas of reef. The shrimp has stout claws and excavates and maintains the burrow, going busily back and forth like a miniature bulldozer. However, it has very poor eyesight and is at risk from predators when engrossed in its building work. So the goby, which has bulging eyes set high on its head, acts as a lookout at the entrance to the burrow. It props itself up on its pelvic fins just outside the burrow entrance so that it can peer all around looking for trouble. In return for the goby's guard duty, the shrimp allows it to live in the safety of its burrow. The two partners communicate by using touch signals. The shrimp lets the goby know when to take up its duties by sweeping its very long, sensitive antennae around until it touches the fish.

1. Ever alert, a goby stands guard while its partner shrimp busily shovels sand from their joint burrow. **1**

If the goby spots a predator (or a diver) when on duty, it swishes its tail from side to side and dives back down the burrow. The shrimp detects these movements with its antennae and it, too, retreats.

Stowaways

The partnership between anemonefish, or clownfish, and giant anemones is on a rather different basis. When early naturalists first observed these charming little fish darting in and out of the deadly stinging tentacles of their anemone home, they simply could not believe their eyes. Some of the inhabited anemones can be up to 1 m (3 ft) across, while the fish are only around 10–15 cm (4–6 in) long. Fish this size and larger are regularly stung and eaten, and yet the clownfish are able to spend their whole lives with their chosen partners, even sleeping at night on the anemone's disc-like upper surface.

So how does the anemonefish 'tell' the anemone not to eat it? Many hours of patient observation by divers and aquarium keepers have partially answered this question. The anemonefish survives by preventing communication between itself and the anemone: it pretends it isn't there. A special mucus covering its whole body makes it 'invisible' to the anemone, which cannot feel, taste or in any way sense the presence of the little fish. This protective cloak is acquired gradually and can be lost if the fish and anemone are separated for any length of time. When the fish first takes up residence in the anemone or returns after being separated, it 'dances' around the anemone, just ▷▷

Previous pages: Some anemonefish are fussier than others about which anemones they will live in. The clown anemonefish from Melanesia uses three different species.

1. A pair of spinecheek anemonefish at home in a bulb-tipped anemone. The male is less than half the size of the female.

1

⭐ The juveniles of some fish live among the tentacles of the Portuguese man-of-war and other powerful stingers.

allowing a few tentacles to brush against its belly fins. Gradually, it increases the contact until it is able to swim right into the anemone, taking anything from a few minutes to a few hours to achieve this.

The question remains as to whether the fish collect the protective mucus from the anemone or manufacture it themselves. There is evidence to support both arguments, and different species of anemonefish may use different methods. Whatever the method, the result is an extremely secure home for the anemonefish, where they can live and breed in safety.

INCREDIBLE JOURNEYS

While anemonefish and others with permanent homes or territories never move far, many oceanic fish undertake seasonal migrations and may travel hundreds or thousands of kilometres every year. These migrations are usually associated with spawning and feeding. The best feeding grounds for fish such as herring and plaice are off shore in deeper water, but the safest place for the young is in shallow inshore areas, so the fish migrate between feeding and spawning grounds.

Mackerel around the British Isles migrate to avoid the worst of the winter cold. They travel long distances to a few specific over-wintering areas in deeper water where water temperatures remain constant. Scientists are able to follow these migrations by catching fish and tagging them before releasing them back into the sea. If the fish is later caught again, it is possible to work out how far it has travelled. One experiment showed that two cod recaptured off the Faroe Islands and Newfoundland had travelled all the way from the North Sea.

From river to sea

These journeys pale into insignificance against the marathon undertaken by salmon. The distances these fish swim, the arduous nature of their journey, and the skill involved in completing it are truly extraordinary. The salmon's life journey begins in the headwaters of freshwater rivers and streams, where the larval fish, called alevins, hatch

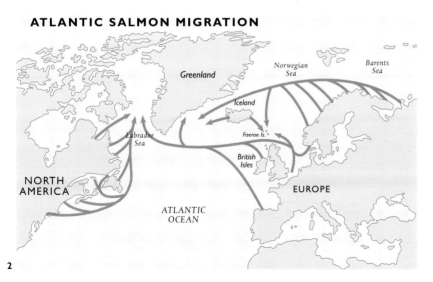

ATLANTIC SALMON MIGRATION

Greenland

Norwegian Sea

Barents Sea

Iceland

Labrador Sea

Faeroe Is.

British Isles

NORTH AMERICA

ATLANTIC OCEAN

EUROPE

2. During their life at sea, many European and American salmon migrate to rich feeding grounds off southern Greenland, Iceland and the Faroe Islands. When it is time to breed, each fish will return to the river in which it was born.

2

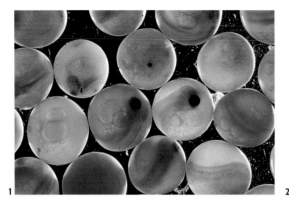

from eggs laid in nests called redds, scooped out of the gravelly river bed. These tiny fish feed and grow into finger-sized juveniles called parr, which have distinctive, dark, camouflage markings like thumbprints along their flanks.

Atlantic salmon parr in northern Europe and North America remain in the upper reaches of their native rivers for one to several years, depending on their growth rate. When they reach a length of 10–20 cm (4–8 in) they instinctively head downstream towards the sea. At the same time,

1. Tiny larval fish inside salmon eggs. When salmon are farmed, the eggs are fertilized and cultured.

2. Atlantic salmon alevins remain in their nest for several weeks.

3. Pacific pink salmon travel up a river in Alaska towards their spawning grounds. After spawning they will all die.

⭐ As long ago as 1653 Sir Isaac Walton marked young salmon and proved that they returned to their home rivers.

they start to lose their baby colours and take on the beautiful, iridescent silvery sheen of the adults, which will provide good camouflage in the open sea. At this stage they are called smolts.

When they reach their river estuaries, most smolts spend some time there adjusting to the increasing saltiness of the water. Most freshwater fish would quickly die if put into salt water, but salmon can adjust their physiology amazingly quickly. Some fish even survive being poured straight into salt water from rivers that plunge directly into the sea. Once at sea, the fish range far and wide, travelling from Europe or America to

Greenland and the edge of the Arctic Ocean. They grow quickly until they reach several kilograms in weight and become sexually mature.

And back again

After spending from one to several years at sea, the urge to spawn starts the salmon off on their long journey home. Each salmon heads back from its distant feeding grounds towards the exact river in which it was hatched. Salmon from North America, the British Isles and Scandinavia may all have been feeding together, but when they are ready to spawn, they will go their separate ways. Travelling back across the ocean towards their home coasts, the salmon probably use ocean currents as directional clues, and may also have some ability to sense the Earth's magnetic field.

As they near their coasts, an acute sense of smell allows the fish to recognize their home coastal

3

1. (opposite) Chum salmon jumping falls in the McNeil River, Alaska. Sometimes fish ladders are provided to help the fish over dams.

2. Pacific pink salmon spawning *en masse* in a North American river. The fish spawn in water so shallow that their backs break the surface.

2

waters and finally their own birth river. However, arriving at the river mouth, the most difficult part of the journey is still ahead: the returning salmon must swim upstream against increasingly strong currents, through rapids and even up waterfalls. Salmon are famous for their spectacular leaps, and can propel themselves up and out of the water with powerful thrusts of their tail. They may have to leap many times before finally reaching the top of the waterfall. In some salmon rivers, the water authorities build fish ladders around particularly difficult obstacles, including dams for hydro-electric schemes.

Eventually, the fish reach the headwaters of the very tributary in which they hatched. On the way, their sense of smell has been vital, but they have very good eyesight and may remember visual landmarks as they travel up the river. This amazing feat of memory is initiated during their first journey down the river, when important sights and smells are imprinted on them.

The end of the road

The extreme physical effort of making a journey like this, and finally of excavating nests, competing for females and spawning, takes its toll on the fish. Pacific salmon all die straight after spawning and their bodies fill the streams and rivers until they rot or are eaten by scavengers. Atlantic salmon drop back down river to calm pools, where some recover and later make their way back to the sea again. Most do die, but some females may survive and return another year to spawn again. The males often use up the last of their reserves competing for females during spawning and almost none survive.

POPULATING THE OCEANS

POPULATING THE OCEANS

In the early 1990s, a Malaysian fisherman from Sarawak in Borneo got the surprise of his life. Fishing in the Samarahan River estuary, he landed a huge, oval-shaped fish with no tail: instead, it had two triangular fins, one on the back and one on the belly near the rear end. Ten men were needed to haul the 300-kg (662-lb) fish on to the bank. They had caught a sunfish, a rare ocean wanderer that had strayed into the river. This single fish would have started life as one egg among 100 million or more laid by its mother, and was possibly the only survivor – until it was caught. Most bony fish populate the oceans by producing huge numbers of eggs to compensate for enormous losses. However, sharks, rays and some bony fish produce only a few eggs or young and exhibit an extraordinary variety of reproductive strategies. Parental care is restricted to a few bony fish. Sharks and rays all abandon their egg cases or young at birth.

Previous page: The embryo inside this dogfish egg case or 'mermaid's purse' can be clearly seen. The long tendrils are wrapped around seaweed to prevent the egg case drifting away.

SHARK STRATEGIES

Whatever their reproductive strategy, all fish have one aim in mind – to ensure the survival of sufficient offspring to maintain their species. Sharks, and their flattened relatives the rays, take a completely different approach from most bony fish: instead of producing huge numbers of eggs at relatively little expense in terms of time and energy, they produce only a few large, yolk-laden eggs or they give birth to well-developed young. This requires a lot of input from the mother but the young have a much greater chance of survival.

Since the eggs start to develop within the mother, it also means that they must be fertilized internally. Unlike bony fish, which can lay eggs that are then fertilized separately by the male, sharks and rays have to mate. The pelvic fins of the males have a pair of hard, rod-like appendages called claspers on their inner edges. During mating, which is generally a fairly violent affair, the male introduces one of the claspers into the female's cloaca, the genital opening. The sperm are neatly packaged in sacs called spermatophores, and these are passed into the female. The males often bite the females in their efforts to get them in the right position for mating. The females are usually larger than the males and tend to bite back, so both may emerge from their embraces worse for wear. Female dogfish, or small-spotted catsharks as they are also known, can store sperm packages for up to two years and this may save them from having to mate too often, as well as allowing them to lay their eggs when conditions are optimal.

1. A pair of stingrays preparing to mate. The smaller male initially follows the female, checking her scent to see if she is receptive.

Mermaid's purses

One of the most rewarding finds for a beachcomber walking a sandy beach after a winter storm is a mermaid's purse. These strangely shaped little brown or black packages are the empty egg cases of sharks and rays. On British beaches, square, black cases with a single projection at each corner belong to various rays and skates. Brown oblong cases with long, tangled tendrils, designed to hold them firmly in the undergrowth, belong to dogfish. Some catshark cases are sculpted with striking geometric patterns. Hornsharks, so called because they have a sharp, horn-like spine in front of each dorsal fin, have beautiful spiral egg cases that they attach to seaweed or sea squirts. The Port Jackson hornshark picks up its egg cases in its mouth and screws each one securely into a rock crevice.

Inside the safety of its horny case, the young shark embryo is nourished by a copious supply of

1. A baby Port Jackson hornshark or bullhead shark emerges cautiously from its spiral egg case, after spending 9-12 months growing and developing inside. The young fish must fend for itself as soon as it swims free.

2. A baby swell shark emerging from its egg case. The young are around 15 cm (6 in) long at birth.

1

2

1. In a shallow, sandy lagoon in Bimini, a baby lemon shark is born tail first. The desire to feed is suppressed in the mother, who might otherwise be stimulated by blood from the birth.

2. Adopting a head-down posture, a titan triggerfish aerates its nest of eggs by blowing water at it.

yolk. It grows slowly, taking a few months to a year to develop. It hatches by cutting its way out of the tough case using specially hardened scales on its head, rather like some birds do with the egg tooth on their beaks. However, unlike baby birds, the newly hatched sharks must immediately look after themselves as their parents are long gone. Public aquariums often hatch dogfish eggs in glass tanks, hanging them up so that they can be clearly viewed. This is an excellent way to see their development, as the egg cases are often semi-transparent.

⭐ Sand tiger shark embryos fight each other in the uterus and the strongest eat the weakest.

Shark mothers

Although many of the smaller shark and ray species lay egg cases, the majority give birth to live young. In the simplest cases, the fertilized eggs simply stay inside the mother, developing and growing by using the food store supplied in their large yolk sacs. They are then born at the same sort of stage as the young of species that have developed in egg cases outside the mother's body. In some sharks, internal development is taken a stage further and the yolk sac and egg membrane fuse with the wall of the uterus and form a type of placenta. The embryonic sharks receive oxygen and nourishment from the mother via an umbilical cord in a manner similar to mammals. Lemon sharks give birth in shallow nursery areas, often in lagoons of seagrass. The newly born pups rest for a few minutes and then swim away, breaking the umbilical connection and immediately taking up an independent life.

DOTING FATHERS

Once their young are born, sharks take no further notice of their offspring and show no parental care beyond not immediately eating them. Most bony fish also have no interest in their eggs after they have been laid, leaving them to drift in the ocean currents, where they develop into free-swimming larvae. There are some notable exceptions to this rule, and some fish guard their eggs assiduously until they hatch. In almost all these cases, it is the male that does the parenting. There are numerous examples, especially among bottom-living fish, and many show great courage and perseverance in carrying out their duties. Divers will always give nesting titan triggerfish a wide berth because these fish have been known to take chunks out of a diver's fins and wetsuit when on guard duty. Even tiny damselfish will try and chase a diver off. Lump-suckers lay their eggs on rocks in shallow water and will stoically grip on to the rocks with their sucker and sit out a battering from storm-tossed seas.

The most extreme example of fatherhood is shown by the seahorses and their relatives. Seahorses are extraordinary in all respects and have long captured the imagination of both scientists and the general public. No marine aquarium is considered complete without a display of these delicate fish. Many Asian countries, such as the Philippines, export large numbers of live fish for this trade. In other countries they are considered magical, and they are widely used in Chinese medicine. All this is bad news for the seahorses, whose numbers continue to dwindle.

2

1

1. Seahorse pairs remain faithful to each other for the duration of the breeding season and possibly for longer.

2. (opposite) A male seahorse giving birth. The young are miniature replicas of their parents and can fend for themselves immediately.

Seahorses have rigid bodies made up of bony plates, and they carry their heads bent over, like a tightly reined-in carriage horse. Their tail is prehensile, being used to hold on to seaweed and seagrasses. Although not fast movers, seahorses are able to swim gracefully using the single fin on their back, and they perform intricate greeting and courtship dances. Courtship may go on for several days until the female is ready to lay her eggs. This she does by entwining herself around the male and depositing the eggs in a special pouch on the male's belly. The male fertilizes the eggs, and in many species the pouch then seals up to protect the eggs. With his bulging belly and upright stance, the male seahorse really does look pregnant. The developing eggs float in a type of placental fluid that is oxygenated by blood capillaries in the pouch wall.

The eggs hatch in the pouch after a few days to several weeks, depending on the species, and the young seahorses, miniatures of their parents, are pumped out of a hole in the top of the pouch. In most cases, that is the end of the father's responsibilities, but in some seahorses, the young return to the pouch whenever danger threatens.

Mouth brooders

In Africa's Rift Valley lakes there exists another group of fish remarkable for their parental prowess. Cichlids are perch-like fish that have diversified into an amazing number of species. There may be as many as 2000 different types, but accurate estimates are impossible because many new species have yet to be described by scientists. In Lake

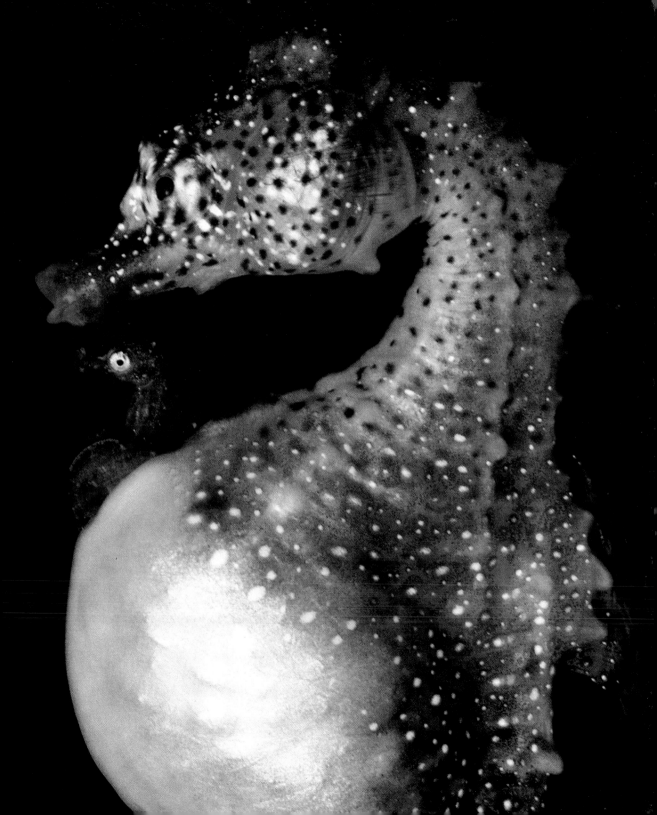

Victoria alone, there are around 300 species, each with a different colour pattern. Most cichlids make excellent parents. The angelfish, a popular freshwater aquarium fish, is a cichlid, although it has an unusual flattened shape designed for camouflage among water plants. It lays its sticky eggs on leaves, which it first cleans with its mouth. The eggs are guarded, and fanned to keep them clean and provide them with oxygen, until they hatch. The tiny fry are also guarded for a while and herded together for safety at night.

The more advanced cichlid species take things a remarkable stage further. When the female has laid her eggs, she carefully scoops them up into her mouth and keeps them there until they hatch. After hatching, the fry are allowed out to feed, but are encouraged back into her mouth at night and when danger threatens. This may go on for several weeks,

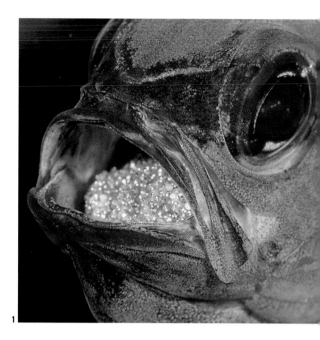

1

▶ SHARKS IN DANGER

Sharks are slow breeders: they produce only a few young at a time, from two in the sand tiger and bigeye thresher sharks, to a maximum of 135 in blue sharks. Many do not reach sexual maturity until several years old, and their gestation period can be as long as two years. All this makes sharks vulnerable to overfishing. Sharks are fished for their meat, oil and cartilage, which is ground up to make medicines. Perhaps the cruellest trade is for their fins (right), used in shark's fin soup: the animals are often thrown back into the sea, still alive but minus their fins. Many shark populations have now been reduced to such low numbers that they will never recover. Recent surveys of fish markets in the Philippines and Malaysia found that the few sharks on sale were mostly juveniles, indicating that even the nursery grounds are now being fished.

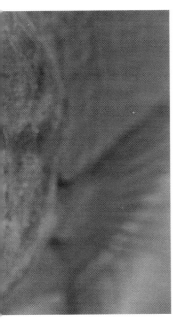

1. The mass of eggs in the mouth of this male ring-tailed cardinalfish can be clearly seen. He will not feed until the eggs have hatched and the fry dispersed.

2. A parrotfish resting on a coral reef in the Maldives. Its protective mucus cocoon is renewed each night.

MALE OR FEMALE?

In most vertebrates – mammals, birds, reptiles and amphibians – the sexes are separate and the animals remain as males or females all their lives. There are often obvious differences in colour, size and other secondary sexual characteristics between males and females. The majority of fish also follow this system, although it is often difficult to tell the sex of a fish from its appearance alone. However, there are a surprising number of fish types in which gender is anything but straightforward, and hermaphrodites are the norm. A hermaphrodite is both male and female at the same time, and this is common in invertebrate animals such as snails. But hermaphrodite fish generally function first as one sex and then later in life change to the other sex. The related wrasse and parrotfish are two examples

and during that time the mother does not feed. Sometimes the male shares the brooding duties, and in some species the male does it single-handed. Unfortunately, many of these remarkable fish are nearing extinction. Introduced predators, such as the Nile perch, have caused considerable havoc, and overfishing and pollution are also contributing to their decline.

Mouth brooding is not restricted to freshwater species: in the sea, cardinalfish also use this method of parental control. Cardinalfish live mostly on coral reefs and are small, nocturnal fish. By day they can be seen hovering quietly in groups under coral heads, or in holes and caves. In this group, it is the males that do the brooding.

2

of fish families in which many of the species undergo a sex change. In most cases the change is from female to male, but in some parrotfish, it is from male to female.

A colourful life

The cuckoo wrasse is one of Britain's most colourful fish. The females are a beautiful rosy red with a line of alternating black and white patches along the top of the tail stalk and part of the back. The males are a bright orange or pink, with dark blue heads and brilliant blue lines and blotches along the sides and on the fins. However, some-times fish are seen that seem to have elements of both these colour patterns. They have the orange and blue colours that normally denote a male, but they also have the black and white patches of the female. This was what first made scientists suspect that the fish might change sex. The large, blue and orange males develop from females some time

★ Bitterlings lay their eggs inside the gill chamber of freshwater mussels. In exchange, young mussel larvae attach to the fish for a free ride to new territory.

between 7 and 13 years. When the change is complete, the newly formed males take up a territory, and in the spring each male will try to entice females to his nesting area with an elaborate courtship dance. If a female responds, he dazzles her even further by blanching completely white over the head and shoulders in just a few seconds, the colour subsequently returning as quickly as it went.

This sex-change system allows as many fish as possible to be female and thus produce lots of eggs and young. Only a few males are necessary to fertilize the eggs. However, this is certainly not the whole explanation: it is now known that not all young cuckoo wrasse are females. Some eggs hatch as males but with the female coloration. These are called primary males and, as far as is known, they do not change colour or become territorial males. In some tropical wrasse, these primary males take part in group spawning with females and may change colour. Larger secondary males that used to be females take part in individual courtship and spawn with one female at a time.

Sexual triggers

Exactly what triggers the sex change in cuckoo wrasse is not clear, but in the small tropical cleaner wrasse, it is controlled by a social hierarchy.

Cleaner wrasse spend their lives manicuring other fish. They set up shop by a prominent head of coral, often called a bommie. Sweetlips and other large fish queue up at their local bommie, spreading their fins and opening their mouths to indicate that they would like a wash and brush-up. The little cleaner wrasse swims fearlessly around the fish, picking off skin parasites and even entering their mouths and gill openings. The cleaner wrasse live in small groups consisting of a large, dominant male and a harem of smaller females. The aggressive behaviour of the male prevents any of the females from changing sex. However, if the male is killed, perhaps by a thoughtless client, or is removed by a curious scientist, then the largest and bossiest female immediately assumes control of the harem.

1. The distinctive colours of this female cuckoo wrasse make it easy to identify.

2. This male cuckoo wrasse has completed his sex change and has lost all traces of his previous female coloration.

3. It is difficult to tell male and female cleaner wrasse apart. Both sexes will pick parasites off larger fish, such as this sweetlips.

3

Her change in behaviour is followed by a physical change of sex, and within a few days she quickly becomes a fully functional male.

A similar system operates with anemonefish, or clownfish, but in this group the sex change is from male to female. These small fish live in 'families' in association with large anemones. The largest and most dominant fish is a female, and her much smaller partner is a male. There will also usually be a number of small, non-breeding fish in the group. If the female dies, the male changes sex and takes over her role. Meanwhile, the largest non-breeding fish matures and takes over the male's role. This system means that if one of the pair dies, the other does not have to wait for a new mate or go out and look for one in the open water where predators lurk.

UGLY BABIES

Most newly hatched fish larvae grow fast and quickly come to resemble their parents. Scientists can identify the young fish from a fairly early age when they catch them in plankton nets towed behind boats. Young eels, however, are so different from their parents that they were originally described as a separate species. Adult eels are long and thin, like a piece of rope, and their shape allows them to wriggle in and out of almost any space. By contrast, the young, known as leptocephalus larvae, are completely flattened and shaped like a willow leaf. It was not until the 1890s that it was proved beyond doubt that the leptocephalus fish developed into young eels. Before this, as no one could find

any baby eels, many people believed they appeared by magic. One traditional story was that the long hairs from a stallion's tail turned into eels when they fell into water.

The shape of the leptocephalus is totally unlike that of the adult eel because these larvae have a completely different lifestyle from the adults. They spend the first few months or years of their lives

2

drifting in the ocean currents, and their flat shape means that they are pushed along faster and do not sink to the seabed. Adult freshwater eels from Europe set out on a remarkable journey when it is time to breed. They make their way down rivers and streams and out to sea, then swim all the way across the Atlantic to the Sargasso Sea, which lies east of the Bahamas and southwest of Bermuda. The eels spawn here in very deep water and then die. The eggs hatch into young leptocephalus larvae, which then begin their long journey home. Scientists have recently worked out that European eel larvae take only 12 months to return to the coasts of Britain. It was previously thought that this took up to three years. As they near the coast, the leptocephalus larvae start to change shape and become elvers – miniature, semi-transparent eels. Finally, the elvers reach the river mouths and make their way upstream and into all types of fresh water.

1. European eels spend up to 20 years in fresh water before migrating to the sea.

2. Young eels are called leptocephalus larvae because they were once thought to be a different species.

3. Adult eels migrate to the Sargasso Sea from rivers all over Europe. The young drift back on currents, such as the Gulf Stream.

3

EEL MIGRATION

Greenland

Iceland

NORTH AMERICA

EUROPE

Gulf Stream

ATLANTIC OCEAN

Sargasso Sea

AFRICA

Flat out

Flatfish are another group of fish that undergo a complete change in body shape between the young larval stage and the adult form. Flatfish hatch from floating eggs as tiny but normal 'upright' fish. Plaice larvae drift with the ocean currents for a few weeks, feeding on minute, shrimp-like animals called copepods. Eventually, they are carried by currents to shallow inshore areas, which act as safe nursery grounds. Now they start to change their behaviour and shape. The young fish frequently swim on their sides, with the left side facing down, and their bodies start to flatten out so that they become very thin from side to side. They now spend most of their time lying on the seabed. The eye on the underside is of no use in that position, so it migrates round until both eyes are on the same side (the right side). The mouth also twists round so that it can be opened more easily. The last change to occur is the loss of colour on the underside, which becomes more or less white. The colour on the top side of the fish provides camouflage, but there is no need for any colour on the underside. By changing in this way, the fish has a body shape suited first to life in the open sea and then to life on the seabed.

1

RIVALS AND PARTNERS

Sex among most fish is a fairly casual affair, often involving mass spawning. During spawning, eggs and sperm are released simultaneously by many fish so that a high proportion of the eggs are fertilized. The time of spawning is controlled by instinct, changes in water temperature and even the phases of the moon. Californian grunions provide one of the most dramatic examples of this type of spawning. They gather together in their thousands, just off shore from specific beaches, two to six days after a new or full moon. Their timing is designed to coincide with the highest tides so that their eggs can be deposited in the sand high up the shore and out of reach of most predators. In such mass spawning there is no need for the males to spend any effort in attracting females as all the fish turn up in the same place at the same time. But species in which the male fish builds a nest and looks after

2

1. This large toothed flounder from Bahrain has its eyes on the left side of its body and lies on its right side. Other flatfish species have the opposite arrangement.

2. Grunion risk becoming stranded on the beach as they swim into the shallows to lay their eggs.

 PERMANENT PARTNERS

Deep-sea anglerfish (right) spend their lives drifting through the dark depths of the oceans. Finding a mate can be a daunting task, but anglerfish have overcome the problem by job sharing. The females concentrate on finding food, using a luminous lure to entice prey within reach of their fearsome teeth. The tiny males, less than 5 cm (2 in) long, have no teeth, so cannot eat. Their sole aim in life is to track down a female by following her scent trails with their ultra-sensitive nostrils. When a male finds a potential mate, he latches on to her with hooks and waits until it is time to spawn. In some species, the male and female tissues join permanently and the male is supplied with food via the female's blood.

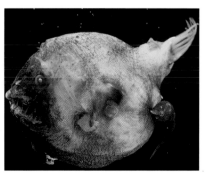

the eggs and young must first entice a female to lay her eggs where he wants them. These males have evolved beautiful, complex courtship dances to entice females to spawn with them.

Nesting fish

In northern European and North American rivers, streams and lakes, the little three-spined stickleback is famous for his eye-catching displays. In spring the male develops bright breeding colours designed to attract females – normally he is silvery, with a dark greenish back and paler belly. As the breeding season approaches, his belly takes on a vivid red colour and his eyes become a brilliant greeny-blue. He then builds a nest, first making a mound of plant material, which he binds together with a sticky

substance produced in the kidneys. When the mound is sufficiently large, he burrows through it to make a hollow, covered nest. The next step is to find an egg-laden female and persuade her to lay eggs in his nest. When he finds a willing partner, he dances in a zigzag pattern, backwards and forwards. The female will follow him to the nest, and if she approves of his handiwork, she will dart in and lay her eggs, followed by the male, who fertilizes them. The display is highly ritualized, and if anything goes wrong, the pair will not spawn.

A rocky retreat

Many species of fish around the world build elaborate nests. Others, such as damselfish, simply clear a patch of rock and perform their courtship

1. Female sticklebacks are attracted to males with the largest red patches.

2. A male stickleback courts a female. Her bulging belly shows that she is ready to spawn.

2

dance over this territory. The bright yellow garibaldi damselfish lives in forests of giant seaweed known as kelp, off the Californian coast. The male clears a patch of everything except red algae (seaweed) and uses this as his nest. Whenever a prospective mate comes near, he displays to her, showing off his swimming abilities by speeding along for a short distance. A successful courtship culminates in the female swimming slowly over the nest area and dropping her sticky eggs on to the rock surface. The male fertilizes them and then tends and guards them until they hatch.

Extraordinary fish

Early seafarers would hardly have believed that fish could exhibit such tender parental care. They thought that the sea was populated with monsters: huge fish with sharp claws and fangs. We now know that the truth is far stranger. What would those sailors have made of a leafy sea dragon or a hammerhead shark? As we explore our seas and fresh waters, new species are discovered. Only careful management of the oceans' resources will allow this wealth of extraordinary fish to survive.

FURTHER INFORMATION

BOOKS

Q. Bone, N.B. Marshall and J.H. Blaxter, *Biology of Fishes* (Chapman & Hall (Thornes), 2nd edition, 1995).
An undergraduate-level reference book on all aspects of the structure and functioning of fish.

Frances Dipper, *British Sea Fishes* (Underwater World Publications, 2nd edition, 2000).
An identification guide to inshore fish likely to be seen by divers, snorkellers and fishermen. Each species is illustrated with an underwater photograph.

Frances Dipper and Anne Powell, *A Field Guide to the Waterlife of Britain*, Reader's Digest Nature Lover's Library. (Reader's Digest Association 1984).
One of a popular series of field guides that provides identification details and interesting information on British species. This guide covers freshwater and marine life, and includes fish.

Samuel H. Gruber (editor), *Discovering Sharks* (American Littoral Society, 1990).
A compilation of short articles on various aspects of shark natural history.

P.S. Maitland and R.N. Campbell, *The New Naturalist Freshwater Fishes of the British Isles* (HarperCollins, 1992).
A fascinating account of the natural history of all the major freshwater fish found in Britain's lakes, streams and rivers.

J.R. Norman, *A History of Fishes*. 3rd edition by P.H. Greenwood. (Ernest Benn, 1975).
Although now a little dated and illustrated only with line drawings and black and white photographs, this classic book is still worth a read and is a source of much detailed information on almost everything to do with fish.

John R. Paxton and William N. Eschmeyer (eds.), *Encyclopedia of Fishes* (Academic Press, 2nd edition, 1998).
Describes all the main groups of fish (freshwater and marine) with details of their main characteristics, life history and many other fascinating facts. Extensively illustrated with underwater photographs and drawings.

Roberta and James Wilson, *Pisces Guide to Watching Fishes: Understanding Coral Reef Fish Behaviour* (Pisces Books, 1992).
A popular guide to the lives and behaviour of coral reef fish worldwide.

MAGAZINE

BBC Wildlife Magazine
A monthly look at wildlife and conservation around the world.

WEBSITE

FishBase: A Global Information System on Fishes
www.fishbase.org

AQUARIA

There are many excellent public aquaria worldwide, where both freshwater and marine fish can be seen. In the UK, visit the London Aquarium, the National Marine Aquarium, Plymouth.

INDEX